Travels

Hibernia / Hawaiki

Sleepless the Poet

BookLeaf Publishing

India | USA | UK

Made with ❤ on the BookLeaf Publishing Platform
www.bookleafpub.in
www.bookleafpub.com

Dedication

To my amazing Aunt Joan, whose boundless curiosity, love of adventure, and deep appreciation for a great story sparked those same passions in me from a young age.

Without your invitation and encouragement to take those trips across the US as a kid, I doubt this book - or the stories within it - would have ever come to life.

Preface

My name is Sleepless, and I've been writing poetry for public consumption for nearly a decade, though privately for twice as long. While my larger work, A Lengthy Introduction, is still in progress and nearing completion, this book serves as a harbinger of sorts, born from two transformative adventures I embarked on in 2024.

The first journey took me to Ireland, where I spent two weeks traveling the island with my wonderful aunt and cousin. We began in Dublin, then made our way through Waterford, Cobh, Sneem, Kerry, and Galway, before concluding in Belfast. Of the twenty-one poems included in this collection, twelve are inspired by this Irish sojourn.

The second adventure brought me to the island of Oʻahu in Hawaiʻi, where I spent just over a week exploring with the guidance of a dear friend and her family, who are native to the area. Starting on the southwest side of the island, we journeyed to the North Shore for most of the trip, wrapping up with a brief stint in Waikīkī before our departure. The remaining nine poems draw from the beauty and complexity of this Hawaiian experience.

The title, Hibernia / Hawaiki, reflects the poetic and historical names of both islands while also underscoring my role as an outsider. Hibernia was a name given to Ireland by the Romans, an external designation rather than one originating from the Irish Celts themselves. Similarly, Hawaiki refers to the ancestral homeland of the Polynesians before their migration across the Pacific, a term carried into Hawaiian tradition. Both names resonate with the idea of viewing a place from the perspective of an observer, invited in but never entirely native.

I was welcomed with remarkable warmth during these journeys, and the poems in this collection aim to capture the impressions, challenges, and transformations I experienced during those times. Written months after the trips themselves, the poems explore the duality of memory and immediacy, of living an experience and reflecting on it later.

I hope this collection brings you even a fraction of the joy and introspection I found in creating it.

Acknowledgements

Ireland

As stated in the dedication, I would not have done this trip without my AWESOME Aunt Joan. She has been my travel inspiration since I was a kid. When I was in third and fourth grade, she took my sister and I across the country on "Edu-Venture" trips: One to the Grand Canyon and the other to Niagara Falls. In 2018, she invited me to be a chaperone on an EF (educational foreign) tour through Italy and Greece. We liked the EF Tour company so much that it inspired her daughter to plan this Ireland trip with the three of us.

To Joan's amazing daughter and my wonderful cousin, Xan, we actually could not have made this trip without you because you were the one who decided to even do it! I feel very lucky to have been considered and invited, and I could not have asked for a better travel partner. You're a radiant, positive energy, and I look forward to any journey with you because I know the full-bellied laughs that will come from us playing off each other's humor.

To Cathal, the EF Tour director, and Declan, the tour bus

driver, who lead us all over the Emerald Isle. There is no doubt in my mind that Cathal is the best tour guide in all of Ireland. The level of history and mythology he gave in every location left me utterly spellbound, and I'm sure he gives the same fantastic detail on his other tours outside of Ireland. Declan was a great counterpart to Cathal, being a bit of a jokester and finding a good laugh when the opportunity presented itself. Every now and then, it was plain to see that even Declan was mesmerized by Cathal's stories. I felt a sense of yearning and pleasure seeing two Irishmen from different backgrounds both revel in their innate appreciation for their homeland.

To Gregory, who befriended us on the tour, along with "Randy with the good hair." Everyone on the trip was a delight, but you two stood out for me, and I hope you're both doing well.

Hawai'i

To my dear friend Candice - Because of you, I had the incredible opportunity to travel to O'ahu and experience the island not just as a visitor but through the eyes of your family and your roots. Thank you for being the bridge that introduced me to our friend group, who accompanied us on the trip, as well as your family. Your friendship has been a gift in more ways than I can count, and this trip was just one of the many reasons I'm lucky to have you in my life.

I am exceedingly grateful to your family, who welcomed me and shared their time, stories, and island with us. I also want to thank Caleb for putting up with my endless "Haole" Shakas and being our unofficial tour guide. He took time out of his day to show us around the island and introduced us to his friends, which was greatly appreciated. Finally, I want to thank Linda for caring for Josie at moments so you and Matt could have free time.

To Bethany and Bruce for introducing us to "Leai", and the laughs that brought us. To Bruce for partaking in the exchange of "honi" with me. To Auntie Max for telling me I could pass for a local and inviting me to her farm on the Big Island. We'll have to make sure we give her a visit next time.

To Jess and Zack for keeping the former roommate bond alive. Sometimes, I can feel detached now that we both have separate living situations, but our ocean talks and beach hangs let me know we'll always be family in some form or another.

1. Dublin, Part I

Welp kids, we did it
Took some time off, but now it's time to hit it
Might've fucked up and fell off cause my wits not so
quick wit it
Since picking up the pen again, this time really felt
different

This time, I can feel the distance

Starting over's never easy
Was just trying to grow a crowd to please me
Threw a few out during my time of "weak knees"
But thinking bout getting back into "weekly's"

Hoping this will make them see me

The way I went out into the world to see things
Went a few places with leaves and seedlings
Came back with memories to grow trees for reading
So greetings

This time from Dublin

Went to the Emerald Isle with my aunt and my cousin

And we had a ball cutting up, laughing and cussin'
We were "good craic" said our tour guide, Pink bus'n

Or at least we like to think he said that
But Cathal was complex, and we're a family who seeks
stats
So we could be misconstruing the feedback
But we were such a hoot, that even he laughed

And boy, didn't he need laughs

Cause being Irish comes with a tough history
One with a lot of losses and not many victories
And he held that knowledge everyday piece-mealing
gifts to me
So that I could learn his story in a way that made sense
to me

And Ireland feels so long ago now
Getting ahead of the curve before we even break ground
Got a lot to unpack and got the pics to back sounds
Made from my mouth as my thumbs write them down

Shit makes me so proud

That I picked the pen back up

Cause starting over's never easy

But it's better than giving up

2. Dublin, Part II

Took some time away, and the longer I stayed,
The more I felt like I couldn't recreate
My words at the same level or pace
I did when my heart would always break

Cause if you're not sad, then do you really mean the
things you say?

See, I want that visceral
I want that good good
I want that shit I used to feel when feeling something
was fucking useful

I want that pain in my chest
The same way it hurt when she left
The same way I read "read"
For weeks on sent texts

You could call it a complex
'Cause this shit is complex
The path to seek "sad"
That lives rent-free in my head

Oh! How the grass is truly always greener!

Guess sayings are said for a reason, change demeanor
To think I want that same hurt as back then, slow
thinker
No longer content with life's content, bad for readers

And if they say they mean it more, does that make them
meaner?

Stood in a park twice the size of Central
Was grasping for straws trying to get that hit filled
With the feeling I had 6 years prior, on bent heels
When I felt alive, standing on Greek hills, shouting
through windmills

Shouting to mend ills

Cause I was broken back then, but now I just sit still
And stare at a page filled
With lines of code
Thinking I made skills, but really I know
That all the gold sealed in that pot and stowed
At the end of the rainbow
Gleams less and less, The older I grow

Making it really fucking hard to muster the full whole
And even though

The view was stunning

All I could catch, was only ever an inkling
A small piece of the larger puzzle created from that
original feeling
A morsel minced, but never meant to beseech the thirst
it was feeding
Yet, there I was

Thinking...

How fortunate was I

To have ever caught

Even only that inkling?

3. Waterford

Sometimes you get what you ask for

If that's the case, then maybe I should wish to be back in
a time where you clash swords
Thinking I'll stand a chance on the back of a horse
In some form of armor and survive war

'Cause I have this misguided ideal that I'm a knight
Looking to bend the knee for a just cause and act sure

Thinking I'll have the ability to add more

But even then...

What a privileged thought to have
I should be grateful for what I have
And where I am
And when I am
And what I know

But lately, I've just been feeling down low
Too slow
Can't seem to muster my usual "get-up-and-go"
I either have the energy with no direction to know

Or the direction with no energy to show
Meanwhile, the work mounts, only adding to the load

And I see less and less of those perfect storms where I'm
able to get both

Definitely not feeling the "growth"

I did however...
Get to feel the sun again, on my skin
For a couple of weeks
Been a while since I felt that warm,
Reminding me how much I missed short-sleeves
Reminding me how bright that light could be
And of course, reminding me

That no matter what, the sun always has to set and leave

Nothing I can do to change that

Just try to find a way to stay in it's light longer before it
fades out
I'll stay out
A little longer
It's dark now, but I'm a little warmer
The walk now, to my room is somber
But my head's high from the sights I harbor

In my chest...

All's well, but is it?

Maybe I'm unwell

Oh well...

You know what they say

"Another day, another sun"

So here's to hoping for another one

4. Glendalough, Part I

Catching a second Fall in the middle of June had to be a
blessing
I love the heat when I'm at the beach, but Georgia
Summers can run right through Thanksgiving
And whether I'm blessed or giving thanks, both are
better when I'm not sweating
So that morning walk through Glendalough, a pillar,
picturesque
Reminding: the cool that prevails lies in whichever path
we are heading

Even in the face of devastation, as their Hibernian
history kept detailing

They had sages and friars who went on to become saints,
aspired
Hearing tale of Christ's forty days and forty nights'
tribulations and trials
So they secluded themselves on mountains and hills

And in caves that surrounded lakes

Or on completely stone isles
Where even the illiterate would build churches, rewrite

books, and copies of the Bible

Pacifists, to a fault,
Frequent Viking raids led to a village...

Becoming something more tribal

5. Glendalough, Part II

I saw someone make a comment to a comet that flew
over us the other day
They said, "See you in 86,000 years. When you return,
we'll be back in caves."
Guess they're not too keen on much progress being
made by the human race
And I couldn't really place blame 'cause some days I'm
feeling the exact same fucking way

See, the thing about hoping is it doesn't carry the same
weight
As those lucky enough to be able to walk by faith

Wish I had a say

Unfortunately, my brain has a mind of its own
Doesn't really listen to me, doesn't really do what it's
told
Loves who it loves, checking the cards,
When everyone knows
I need to quit trying to go "all in"
And learn when it's time to give up and fold

But that's the price you pay for staying in and holding

out hope

You seem to think I'm still against it
And disrespectful

Though, I've changed my tune for a while now
Maybe it's easier if you think me less amicable

Less open to hear you out
Though, I'd love to hear you out
Love to learn more about
What you believe 'cause what you believe might be able
to help me out
And quell this dread in my head somehow
Since that motherfucker won't listen to a word I shout

But we both know taking the time for me to hear your
side
Isn't something you're really about

Wonder how the last Druid felt when St.Patrick came
along
Convincing Pagan high kings to make Roman Catholics
of their throngs
And maybe this Druid loved a girl,
One he found his time with to be fond
But he believed in the Sun, and she believed in the Son

And for some reason, one of those was wrong

And maybe "wrong" is a little harsh
But him not believing what she believed did push them
apart
Though, he was willing to learn about the Son as long as
it was taught from her heart
Because it was her that he trusted,
But she never found the time to start

So his love for her became myth,
And through the years, inspired sparks

Until it was painted in a cave 86,000 years into the dark

6. Tír na nÓg

I often wonder what a younger Cam would think of me. Him at 18, and me as I am now, are so different. Not sure he'd doubt the benefit and be pleased with me.

"We got a six-pack yet?"
"We're getting there." I'd say
"Have we ever had a six-pack?"
"You know, we came really close a couple of times, but it wasn't something I could make stay."

"Well, what about a beard? Can we grow a full beard yet?"

laughing
"This answer might be something you hate,
But yes, we can grow a beard.
Though, it doesn't really look like anything you would want to keep on your face."

"Well, what about the band? What about A Ways Away?"
"The band never works out, and neither do any of the other bands you make."
"So wait, what do I do for work then?"

"You're a project manager for a prominent credit card company and bank."
"I'm a fucking suit?! How could we end up this way?"

"Hey, it's not all bad!
You make good money, and they let you have a sleeve and finger tats."
"Oh shit, we got tats?"
"We got tats, boyyyyy!!"

"Okay, okay, not all bad. Did we end up getting the 3 Xs?"

"Nooo, we're not straight-edge anymore. Haven't been for a really long time."
"Wait, you broke edge?! No, we can't be the same guy."
"Well, you'll find out in a couple of years when your gf breaks up with you, and you just want to give up and die."
"She breaks up with me?! No, that has to be some kinda lie."
"'Fraid not kid. But you learn there are other girls out there to find."

"Okay...wait, what happened to being an actor? Did you give up on that too?"
"Well, we spent college getting a degree in film that,

currently, we never use."
"Wow. The tats are cool, but other than that, you sound
like you suck, dude."
"Hey, I know it's hard to hear, but I did the best I could
do."
"Idk, sounds like an excuse.
I mean, you're telling me:

    1. We don't make it in a band,
    2. Or become a famous actor.
    3. We work for "the man."
    4. We broke edge,
    5. AND our gf dumps us...

That's, like, the opposite of everything I am now."

"Yeah well, I always thought this wouldn't really be good
news for you, should this convo ever go down...
But it's really not all bad.
You end up having some really great moments because
of who you are now."

"Yeah? How?"

"Since the bands never work out, you start rapping, and
through that, you make poetry a focus,
And social media really takes off, so much so, that people

make vids and are paid to post it.
So you have a lane to take, though you haven't made it
yet, you have a few folks in your corner who know it.
You kept many of your same friends while making new
ones because making friends was always our
superpower; you chose it.

"Ok, so on our way to becoming a famous poet?"

"Yeah, but after you break edge and break up with a few
more people a few more times,
You learn maybe it's not about fame but instead, clearing
your heart and mind,
From the rage that you know so well, even better than
me, 'cause I've had years now to let that shit subside,
But you learn being angry isn't cool, and it doesn't even
come close to how cool it is to being fucking kind."

"Whateverrrrr, I'm not angry all the time.
I can be nice, I can be kind."

"Just wait for the reality check that's coming when you
don't have her to fall back on.
Or when you actually have to work for something
instead of giving up and finding reasons to pass on,
Or when you lose all the money your film company
made and are left with only a few videos to laugh on,

Or when you find out you and mom were more alike
than you wanted, so you kept her legacy alive by finding
a steering wheel to crash on."

"Sounds like life starts to lose its passion…"

"You go through ups and downs, as everyone does.
I'm not trying to bum you out; I just want you to
understand the why and the because.

I'd tell you not to ever drink, but the way you learn,
You either swim or sink,
And I think there're some people you may never meet,
If you don't make the same mistakes and overcome
them."

"Do I need to meet more people?
I have Genesis 4, Rob Mob, Dan Squad, Hallway
Hooligans…
I have friends."

"Piece of good news is you do a great job of maintaining
a lot of those friendships throughout the years,
But you also make some new ones along the way that
are just as strong as those you have here.
You meet a friend who pushes you creatively and
another who helps you understand your fears.

And this friend has lots of friends, and brings you into
the groups she holds dear.

"Ok, I love hearing that I have more friends. But where's
the romance?

Do
We
Ever
Love
Again?"

laughs
"Yes, we love again. You'll see.
Or maybe you won't.
Guess it depends on how much this conversation affects
things,
And if you decide to do it all differently.
But I hope you don't
'Cause I don't know how time all flows,
But I know I'd be sad if I woke up one day and she was
someone I didn't know...
Or remember."

"Yeah, but if you never remembered her, then how would
you even know to be sad about it?"

"Well...I'd just know.
And that's something you'll understand when you're no
longer 18 and, instead, 33 years old."

face palms
"Fuck me, at 33, we're still emo as hell, aren't we?"

"ITS NOT JUST A PHASE!"

7. Brú na Bóinne

I look up, and there you are staring back
Like you always do, like you always were
Guess you never took your eye off me, though I'm not
sure if that's a fact
Shit with my neck and this shoulder seem to be getting
worse
But it's all just more superficial crap
Nothing's really wrong, 'cept the usual plaguing from
the same old curse:
An overactive mind creating a hypochondriac,
Who never feels satisfied with the image that the mirror
seems to return

My whole life, why have I always been just a little bit
off?

So close, yet so far, can't ever seem to be anything I want
And I eat healthy,
And I lift heavy
To get closer, but it never stops,
These thoughts of inadequacies like, "I thought I was"

Yeah, I bet you thought...

I often wonder if you're humbling me 'cause the type of
person I'd be without my faults:
Narcissistic...
Egotistical...
All the buzzwords for all the bad traits, I'm glad I'm not
But it'd be really cool if you could bring back the
symmetry of which I've sought

Tired of looking at myself, feeling like I'm missing
pieces...

I didn't even know were lost

8. Cobh

Feel like I've been in a cloud lately...
Like I know what I have to do, but not really quite how
to do it
So, instead of putting one foot in front of the other,
I'm finding distractions of procrastination instead of
actions that pursue it
Watching the time on the clock whittle away
While I waste another day, feigning incongruence
"Use it or lose it," they say
But what happens when you stop believing in the words
you tell yourself that motivate and make you do it?

Feels like I'm trying to fit a circle through a triangle
But I'm too obtuse to find the right angle
Too acute, the solution isn't able
So, to make it work, I push through the table
And get the pieces stuck, pleased like I'm capable

When really, I've only made the mess more tangle-able

I read some writing this past week that was inspiring, to
say the least
Let me know how shallow my words can be
And how if there's a metaphorical drawing board

My shit could stand to see -
The pencil and the eraser, before placing it down in
whichever colored ink,
Thinking just because I painted it gold...
That shit don't stink
So, now I'm gonna go do these stretches 'cause I said I
would
I'm gonna go lift some heavy things and put them down
because I said I would
I'm gonna drop these pictures on these pages and finish
this fucking book because I said I would
And I'm going to sit in front of that screen until I feel
good about my job because I said I would

I'm tired of feeling subpar
In my heart
And with my art

So, it's time to up the bar
Get it moving
And find that fucking start

So, I'm gonna go find that fucking start

9. Ring of Kerry

Can I hide here just for a little while?
Before I'm beckoned back to burn alongside the
fluorescent white lights and the ceiling tiles
Before I have to play another game of some kind
Whether it's the job, or the dates, or the friendships I
reconcile

Can I sit here and breathe for only just a little while?

Let the mist in on every molecule of my skin
So, when the wind wraps around me
It sends relief to the burnt ends
And for a split second, I can actually forget
About this fire, within
So, I can exist, atemporal
No longer beholden to the clock's incessant "tick"

Adolescent wish
Ignescent switch

Fueling the hot air to help me reach the dreams, I think,
so big
Creating the means by building steam through another
check placed on a never-ending list

But never letting me sleep, because time will forever be
"always of the essence" type shit

Except for right now...

Listening to these sounds...

The way the water falls, and is carried down and around

Past me and my problems

It was a good moment felt throughout

A secret hidden in a forest

I felt like telling you about

10. Sneem

I forgot I climbed a mountain in 2024
Oh, how quickly they forget
But climbing mountains can be more about life's lessons,
Than the physicality of how hard the real ones actually
hit
Got so much shit on my plate for 2025
Really hoping I'm not making 720p resolutions just to
turn them into 1080p regrets:
Shooting for the stars again, like I did with Dapper
Gentleman, just to fuck it up and see all my mistakes
recreated in hi-def

That took me years to come back from

Financially
Mentally
Emotionally

Left such a bad taste in my mouth; it took away my
entire love for movies

I still watch them
And I still like them
But not like I used to

But that's the beauty of life
One day, that love may come back
After I have a few more wins on my plate
And a lot less setbacks
A lot more fat stacks
To grease the hands of the metaphorical ref
Now calling first-downs instead of audible snaps
That lead to quarterback sacks
'Cause life is what you make it
But with Lady Luck, there's less cracks
You pay less tax
"Oh, right this way sir, no reservation needed when you
know Chef Jacques."
Knowing I been had it
But y'all ain't know I really got it like THAT
Signing my name at the end of 275 pages to put Sleepless
on the map

It's a wrap

Except it isn't yet
All that hoping and dreaming and chest-puffing
Currently exists solely in my head
And I learned from 2016
So I won't wind up in the same mess
With the same debt

Saw this mountain outside the village, Sneem
And tracked down the path 'cause climbing that bitch
was some shit I really said

And then really did...
Putting my actions where my mouth is
Got some big plans for 2025

So here's to climbing more mountains

11. Cliffs of "More" (Moher)

We were consistently reminded of how lucky we were

Ireland was not usually this sunny
So, seeing the Inis in the distance was a treat that doesn't
normally occur

I was riding high off my mountain hike
Ready to walk to the ends of the Earth
Or at least as much as was permitted
During our "not nearly long enough" designated amount
of time to research

So there I was

Standing at the Cliffs of Moher

Shoulda been head over heels, but couldn't help but feel

Like I wanted more

The sight was legendary, but the pictures, ordinary
I wanted more

The moment, relished with my family, but wished my

friends weren't absentary
I wanted more

I felt so alive in Greece and Italy, but I was more tired
here. What was wrong with me?
I wanted more

Our allotted time was mandatory, which adversely made
me a mandatary
I wanted more

Why was it that I didn't feel fully whole?
Like the colors weren't as bright as they were back then
Had my many travels finally taken their toll
My life, no longer the war it was like when I worked
back in the kitchen
These days, my streets were all painted gold
Bought and paid for by myself - once I decided to start
making good decisions

So, then tell me why I wanted more
Standing at the Cliffs of Moher

When I was living the dream I once dreamt of living...

12. Belfast

I'm amassing wealth
Like Edward Lhuyd: Belfastian Welsh
Yet I'm annoyed
That my artistic pursuits again avoid
The fame and fortune, so elusive and coy
The abuse I employ

So when I hit the iceberg and sink
The alloy from my titanium hull, destroyed
And the masses think
"My god, what an awful thing to happen to that poor
boy!"
Yet their sorrow's my joy
'Cause in these parts, baby, you're dealing with the Real
Mccoy
So, my demise was a real decoy
To be written about forever in infamy
So the money is still void
But I'll have made it into the history books
Meaning the fame is ensured
All the way from Atlanta to Charleroi
I'll be falling off the tongues of the Bourgeoise
No more of this Hoi Polloi

I'll be the kid
The GOAT
The Golden Boy

A wish
A ghost
A fortune told

I'll be what's read right before bed
So the kids can dream big
Before they grow old
And wake up

To find their dreams are sold

13. O'ahu

Drip pens soften the skin
What a waste of ink and paper this has all really been

Back to the drawing board, I suppose
A change of scenery ensures everyone grows
And everyone knows
That islands are more fun
When you have a beach to lay on and can play in the sun
Where the poke ran plenty, and the laughs weighed a
ton
And you have a little Josie girl who's finally turning one!

Hats off to the Hawaiian homies for showing me their
homies
I'm sure my shakas were annoying, but couldn't miss the
chance bestowing
Every surfer and local I saw, until the two fingers were
throwin'
Back in my direction, confirming what we were all
knowing

I'm Haole as fuuuuuuuck lol

I wanted it too bad; story of my life

But thankful nonetheless to them Fish N Grillz guys
To Caleb and Candai for being our guides
A trip you talked about making with your friends for
years
So happy it was realized

So happy I was able to come along for the ride

Landing in O'ahu, I found a sense of purpose
Many hands make light work, so how many hands can a
Cam make work it?
Sights on sights on sights - we were gonna make these
seven days worth it
Hope this trip turns out to be the first of many

Because with this one

We only scratched the surface

14. Kapolei

You'd be surprised that even in paradise, you can still find "tent cities"
On the West Side of the island where, more homeless can be found sitting
In front of their beach-front property, taking up sand and littering
But who's really to blame for the poverty when it costs a fortune to afford the living?

Some would say you may be better off dead then
And how come the "west side" of anything is rarely a place you want to spend?
From the West Bank of Gaza to, at one point, Atlanta's West End
Though since, Black Rock moved in, and has been slowly raising all the rent

With our own tent city growing...
Better to be broke on a beach than under a bridge

You can't forget life's silver linings
They're put in your life for when all the gold stops shining
Like the mountains in the background, best believe I'm

thriving
Thinking about climbing
Like I did in Sneem; same shit, different island

And I want that fame and fortune
But not if the price to pay is losing myself
Being reminded by inter-joined cardboard forts can
Send sobering thoughts of how one wrong move can
take away all that wealth
So I'm working to get my piece of the pie all cut into
portions
'Cause when I eat, the homies eat - highlighting their
skills and paying them well

So when I die and meet the maker's retortion
Asking how did I live my life, I can say

I was just trying to help

15. Shark's Cove

It wasn't long before I saw my first Hawaiian sunset
Santorini said theirs was better, so please, Greece
Don't be upset

But the rays on display at the end of every day
Would make bank on the odds, given the parlay
So there's no doubt in my mind
No dilemma, no say

If the dispute is "who has the best sunset?"

Without question, Hawaii's winning the whole bet

It'd be nice to be back on that beach, at Shark's Cove,
overlooking the coast
Bright-eyed and bushy-tailed at the beginning of the trip
Prior to the inevitable and oncoming "end of trip" woes
Or instead of being back at home, behind a desk, staring
out a window
Clicking and typing away
Hoping the work I do somehow makes my position grow
Makes my paycheck show

Me

Why...

Why I'm wasting away with this lower back pain
Instead of selling everything I own
Traveling the globe, living off adventure
Fulfilling my heart and soul

They say patience is a virtue, and I swear I'm trying to be
patient
I'm trying to follow the rules from the plan I made
So I don't take all this effort and waste it
These "no-sugar" days and lifting the weights
So, in the mirror, I can face it
But let's face it
Some days, the anger never dissipates
And I can't find a way to erase it

Why am I even angry at all?

Angry because there is never

Ever

Enough time...

To sleep

To work
To speak
To flirt
To grieve
To hurt
To think
Of her...

Always gotta keep it pushing
Always gotta say, "It's nothing"
Always end up fucking rushing
Always end up losing something

Always fucking counting chickens
From eggs of stone or carved from pumpkins
That'll never hatch, but keep me thinking
They look the part, so change is coming

Maybe that's why I'm angry...

Because there really is enough time, I just find a way to
waste it
Doom-scrolling and pacing, I'm the king of
procrastination
Or making a weird comment at the end of a great
conversation
This is why we can't have nice things

Because if it looks expensive, I'll break it

And then I'll fix it
Hot glue and duct tape it

It'll depreciate in value
So I'll spend more time trying to raise it

Though it will never be the worth it was
But at least it's whole again, so I'll take it

And set it on top of a shelf where every glance

May remind me to be patient

16. Waimea Bay

Well, this is it, folks…

Throwing my hat in the ring, and I'm going for broke
Wishing the future was something I've seen
So making the right move was something I did know
Staring at these posters in this Air BNB
With the slogan tagged under saying, "Eddie would go"

Standing on this land, ancient and prehistoric
Planning on making purchases for future Cam to adore it
On Downtown escapades and Endeavors to assure it
I ain't never trying to be 2nd place, call me All Might,
I'm meteoric
And I'm for it
I love seeing my city grow, so getting in on the ground
floor's euphoric
Writing in riddles with red herrings and metaphors
To keep folks either guessing or ignoring
The shit I say so I don't take
This confidence and mistake it for clairvoyance
Placing my eggs in blankets to stay warm
And hatch fast, and not counting a single one before it

Keeping my head down till I see that fifty-footer

Grabbing my board, paddling out
And whatever happens, I'll absorb it
And if, in the end
It chews me up and spits me out
Then that's the price I pay for moving forward

'Cause standing still and staying in the same place
Ain't how you get slogans on posters that people can say
In motivational posts to lift them and claim
How the motions of ghosts could help them feel brave

So....

If "Eddie would go"

Then I'm doing the same

17. Pu'u o Mahuka Heiau

It was here I felt like I could finally breathe again

Somewhat ironic since we were surrounded by graves of people
Who would no longer breathe again
Except, maybe now they did; they were just breathing in a different sense
Perseverating long enough for us to stand and peak through these trees with them

I'll never pretend

To know what comes after

We had just raced the sun to catch this view
So whatever happened next didn't really matter

For once

 I was finally present

But only for a moment

As the sky grew more caliginous

I knew our time here was short, but sooner than
expected
We were finished
Our next adventure already underway
As we piled into our two-car caravan, with a quickness
We knew the park rangers would lock the gate
The thought of getting trapped or stranded was a
hindrance
Because getting back to the place we stayed...
If we had to walk, would be a distance

So I inhaled a breath to take it all in

Thankful for my choices and the decisions I did

To get to that moment and share it with friends

What a gift I've been given...

This life that we live

18. North Shore

This project consumes me

Until I've crossed the finish line, the other pieces of the
pie
Have been reduced significantly
Venturing into uncharted territory
Attempting to write four poems in a single day could
end most dubiously
Running the risk of things beginning to sound the same
With reoccurring rhyme schemes and my moderate but
limited vocabulary
So...
How do we proceed?

I must be devoured

Enveloped by the flow I seek
Which can sometimes take hours
Reach into the depths of me
And find these thoughts; obscene and soured
Until the words all exude and bleed
From my pores, like sweat empowered
And they're printed on this page to feed
My hunger and thirst that scours

And ravages

Like the airborne salinity found across yards of salvages
Establishing nominal damages managing
To prove positive on human skin
But on our metallic counterparts, they're savages

Though, sometimes, I never find the flow
And can only eke out passages

A few at a time

Needing an aggressiveness

That only turns out pacifist

19. Hale'iwa, Part I

A beauty birthed like no other
You, the Sun, and I, the Moon

Only at our passings of dawn and dusk
Are these cherished moments when I see you

And our time is short, but my spirit flutters
As the clouds cascade down and fill the view

Until they're far beyond our tranquil ocean
Lost to the darkness of tomorrow's hue

"And for how long will I have your love?" you ask

"For forever, I swear it's true"

"How can you be so sure, with candor?
Forever's a long time to let love accrue"

"Yes, you're right, my darling Sun
With your rays so bright while your warmth bestrews

But even without our lovely banters,
It's plain to see there's none like you"

"Well, there's plenty of suns out there, I'm sure
From many more that you could choose"

"I'm sure there are, but why go looking?
When I've found the one I want, my search is through"

"Because one day my light will be extinguished
So how will you love me then? What will you do?"

"Then, you can follow me into the dark
Where I've been alone and waiting

Waiting to be joined

And reunited with you"

20. Hale'iva, Part II

Remind me, again, what it was like to be a kid
You see, the older I am, the easier it becomes to forget
Playing Manhunt, or Tagalong, or some other game that
we'd invent
Our imaginations were untamed
And now caged
From all this five to nine bullshit

Earlier, I was driving in the snow
Missing those sunny days we had on O'ahu's northern
coast
Thinking 'bout how I used to yearn for the walk but
didn't care about where we'd go
As long as I was with the homies, though sometimes, I'd
even walk alone

I wanted the adventure

And I couldn't sit still

I guess I haven't changed in that regard

The same can't be said for my kind of thrills

They're more expensive now
And take planning to build
But the payoff is more grand
Than it was before I paid bills

Or at least that's what I tell myself
To make it all not feel as bad
But back then, I felt more free
And now, I'm definitely more sad

And if I let it, these thoughts will destroy me
So, dwellings got nothing to add
Instead, I'll focus on the positives
Remembering, fondly, all the good times we had

21. Waikīkī

If you're ever feeling down with your travel gang consort
From "last day blues," just hit a Waikīkī resort
Day pass for the win before catching rides to the airport
Saying bye's always hard, but easier with a pool to
cavort

From here, I'm off to the Tennessee mountains
To witness matrimony with love compounding
And boundless layovers forecasted ahead
But that's a tale for another book
With this one at it's end

So goodbye

Aloha

Au revoir

And slán

Thank you again to our hosts
Who allowed us to come along

As some friends I have like to say

"We'll be seein' ya soon"

Whether that's whenever you come to see us

Or whenever we come back to see you